AJCUNA

Reflections on Finding Harmony with the Universe and with Oneself

MARCIN KOZAKOWSKI

Copyright © 2024 by Marcin Kozakowski

All rights reserved. No part of this publication in print or in electronic format may be reproduced, stored in a retrieval system, or transmitted in any form or by any means, electronic, mechanical, photocopying, recording, or otherwise without the prior written permission of the publisher.

The scanning, uploading, and distribution of this book without permission is a theft of the author's intellectual property. Thank you for your support of the author's rights.

ISBN: 978-1-64704-894-5 (hardcover)
ISBN: 978-1-64704-893-8 (paperback)
ISBN: 978-1-64704-895-2 (eBook)

CONTENTS

Introduction. v

Chapter 1 – Africa First Calling 1

Chapter 2 – Gozo Island 5

Chapter 3 – Back in Poland 7

Chapter 4 – First Excursion to South Africa. . 11

Chapter 5 – Londolozi Game Reserve. . . . 19

Chapter 6 – Namibia. 25

Chapter 7 – Moremi Game Reserve 33

Chapter 8 – Being Back in Poland 41

Acknowledgments 43

Author Biography 45

INTRODUCTION

I deeply believe there is beautiful life awaiting each of us. A life of authenticity, inner integrity, and harmony with Greater Intelligence. If we are willing to cooperate with the Universe, which is constantly communicating with us through the inner landscape of our body and surrounding environment, and we choose to make ourselves sensitive and attentive to be able to learn that language, we are on a good path to harmonizing our life.

This book is a record of the process of transformation from an inauthentic life rooted in a lack of healing to a life that is more peaceful, harmonious, and filled with purpose. It will take you through an external adventure and internal calling from the deepest part of my soul that I was invited to answer.

CHAPTER 1

AFRICA FIRST CALLING

I have never consciously thought of going to Africa. If someone told me even a year earlier that I would have already made two excursions to South Africa, that Africa would be knocking at my heart and soul so vividly, and that my yearning to go back there would be so strong, I probably would not have given it too much attention or believed it. At that time, I was thinking that after selling my apartment in Warsaw, Poland, I would buy a piece of land in the south of Poland and settle in. But life had a different plan for me.

Africa slowly started to appear in my thoughts during the last stages of a challenging and transformative period of my life in Warsaw. For many years, I may have seemed externally happy, but the truth was that, internally, I felt disconnected from the most natural and authentic parts of myself. I was working for an international company that maintained the image of something that could be considered an external success. The problem was that, although it served a very good purpose of supporting researchers and libraries, I have never truly felt that a sales role was for me. Year after year, I was moving away from something that would fulfill, energize, and sustain my adventurous spirit. I knew that to start introducing changes, I needed to create some space between my life at that time and my ability to replenish my vital forces and catch some distance from the challenges I was facing. Despite having a deep, inner conviction that I wanted to leave the company and travel on my own, for some time I lacked the courage to take that step, uncertain of how things would unfold. I started to look for places in the world where I could find some relief and I found one on Lesvos Island in Greece. This gave me the sufficient energy, decisiveness, and courage to commit to leaving the company and following my inner conviction with tangible steps. On that life-supporting wave of energy, I prepared my termination of employment and announced it to my manager. My heart was beating much faster than usual, but once we had an honest conversation, I felt such relief. After that moment, the process of leaving the company lasted several months, as I couldn't and didn't want to leave immediately. It was gradual, collaborative, and gentle. This decision, as I look at it now, has affected the entire course of my life from that point onward.

The following years were filled with numerous workshops, individual healing sessions, exploration of different modalities, meeting many people in Poland who are dedicated to their healing, and supporting others in that matter. I was also searching for the next trustworthy and experienced allies who would sincerely support me in my healing endeavors. Although I was gradually becoming aware that I was losing my precious energy in the environment where I lived, I spent most of the year struggling with letting go of my familiar life and making the decision to sell my flat. The process of readiness lasted for a few months before I was able to sign the agreement and hand it over to the new owner.

CHAPTER 2

GOZO ISLAND

Gozo, for reasons unknown to me at the time, had been knocking at my door for some time. It started to appear from various directions, signaling that there was something important for me to experience on the island. As I learned a little later, Gozo served as a platform for what was about to happen next. I didn't think it was a superficial desire I could treat lightly, but rather very specific guidance that I was receiving. Soon after I found myself in Gozo, I began to experience something beautiful, both internally and in the surrounding environment. The dreams that I had and the environment around me started to communicate with me in a direct and understandable way, in the same manner as it had pointed me to Gozo a few weeks earlier. This time, the guidance was clear that the next destination should be South Africa. Despite receiving so many signs and guidance, I couldn't understand why something in me was resisting the idea of flying to Africa.

One day, while on the other side of the island, I drove to the nearest town to take a walk and have lunch. Once I was in the restaurant, I pulled out my notebook and began writing some reflections from the day. At that moment, an English-speaking couple came inside and sat at the table next to me. A few minutes later, the man turned to initiate a conversation with me. With a little smile on his face, he asked, "Is this the book that you are writing there?"

CHAPTER 3

BACK IN POLAND

During my time in Warsaw, after speaking with a friend of mine, I was inspired to visit the Warsaw Zoo. I wanted to see lions, so when I arrived, I meandered along the pathways, hoping to find them. After a while, I arrived at small, rocky area, which was the current home of the lions. Unable to see any lions, I decided to return to my car and drive back home. I took a beautiful photo of a sculpture of a lying lion and headed back toward the exit. After a few steps, I heard a massive, echoing roar from within the rocks. Immediately, the strength of it woke me up. It was a sound of power, enormous potential, presence, and majesty, yet also a sound that, to me, felt like sadness and longing for freedom. I noticed that none of the people around me, at least to my perception, seemed to hear it. How was that possible? Were these people asleep while being awake?

Soon after Christmas Eve and New Year's, I decided to drive to Lower Silesia. One reason was that I couldn't find a place in Warsaw; another was that it had stayed with me since I had lived there before for a few months. The third reason was that, as I was still on the island instead of going to South Africa, I signed up for few days of an intensive workshop focused on soul retrieval. Soul retrieval is a very subtle process that needs to be protected and cared for. It focuses on the parts of ourselves that left us during difficult experiences. The process involves various rituals, deep heartfelt commitment, purity of intention, solitude, and, most importantly, working with someone who is trustworthy. It must be performed with someone who works with sincere intention, professional preparation, sufficient experience, and support from unseen realms. The workshop, held amongst so many people craving healing in such a beautiful and supportive place as Antoniow, was an experience that left me with a sense of fulfillment, empowerment, and nourishment.

My time in Antoniow, a beautiful mountain village in the south of Poland, was also a time of seeing that the idea of buying a piece of land and settling in was no longer alive in me. The calling to travel and explore South Africa was so strong, and it became clear that this was not the path for me. My energy, focus, and time were dedicated to the process of healing and preparing for my excursion. Knowing that I would be visiting the Londolozi Game Reserve in a few months gave me an additional boost of energy, motivation, and resources to continue moving forward. I left Antoniow, driving through the open, beautiful, and already sunny vast landscapes of Lower Silesia with a deep sense of gratitude. At that time, I didn't know if I was ready, but I knew it was time to courageously step into what life was calling me toward. A few days later, after purchasing a ticket to Johannesburg and confirming my bookings for the first week in South Africa, with my heart beating much faster than usual, I was finally going to Africa.

CHAPTER 4

FIRST EXCURSION TO SOUTH AFRICA

I cannot say that the days between purchasing the ticket and taking the flight to Johannesburg were easy and calm. I felt quite anxious, and my mind raced with doubtful and fearful thoughts as I tried to anticipate the future. The inner turmoil and anxiety settled down after two or three hours into the flight, allowing me to relax and sink into a reflective and contemplative mode that I truly enjoyed. When I landed at the Johannesburg - OR Tambo International Airport, I was a little bewildered and tired as I made my way to customs. At the official information desk, I met a young woman who helped me arrange a taxi and walked me to the parking lot.

As we neared my destination, I asked the driver to pull over so I could withdraw some money. As I was doing that, I sensed a strange, immediate presence around me, as though some restless spirit was nearby. A few seconds later, out of the corner of my eye, I noticed a man walking towards me in a hurried manner, as if he intended to rob me. But at the last second, he changed his mind, lowered his head, and disappeared around the corner. My heart was racing.

The plan for the next three days was to rest after the trip, absorb the spirit of President Mandela's former house, and move to a wildlife sanctuary to see lions. On the second day, I began looking for a car rental company nearby. The owner was kind enough to offer to bring the car

FIRST EXCURSION TO SOUTH AFRICA

to my hotel, so we could arrange everything there. On the day of my departure, the man arrived in the morning, we signed the necessary documents, and he handed me the keys, setting me up for the adventure ahead. Around two hours later, I arrived at the beautiful and wild area home to a wildlife sanctuary neighboring the Dinokeng Game Reserve—the closest natural and well-maintained wildlife ecosystem to Johannesburg and Pretoria. Driving through the open and vast landscape along the red gravel road, I entered a complex of natural land surrounded by a beautiful mountain range and took a deep breath. My entire being responded to that environment.

It was around that time, surrounded by miles of wild bush, that I began taking early mornings seriously—not only waking up early, but also taking care of the important areas of my well-being first thing after rising. I am sure my commitment played a role, but I also felt that the environment helped me tremendously. I had many ideas and expectations for how I would spend these few weeks in South Africa, but one of the main things that happened upon my arrival was that I completely slowed down on all levels. The longer I stayed, living simply in a wooden cabin with direct exposure to the wilderness, the more I felt harmonized with nature's pace. I moved slower and thoughtfully. I was not rushing anywhere. I took time each morning to exercise, sit in silence, and feel the emotions present within me. As much as possible, I read a few pages each morning. My nervous system was slowing down, and I gradually began to feel more present.

Around a week later, I moved to a camp on a hill, and the energy started to change. I concluded that I wanted to fully

FIRST EXCURSION TO SOUTH AFRICA

experience the bush, witness wildlife, and engage in the experience of tracking. I began searching for a place that could provide such an experience. The camp I chose was in the middle of the Manyeleti Nature Reserve, which borders the Timbavati and Sabi Sand Nature Reserves. Within two or three days, everything was organized, and I was ready to depart. Upon my arrival, I was warmly welcomed by the camp staff, the guide, and the tracker, who later became my daily companions on bush walks and game drives. It took me a little time to settle in and rest after the journey, but as soon as I was ready, we jumped into the safari vehicle and headed into the bush. Soon after we left the camp, I saw an entire pride of lions for the first time in my life. The pride included one huge male, one younger male, three or four lionesses, and several cubs, all busy eating the remains of a giraffe they had hunted the night before. When leaving the camp, I had hoped to encounter these animals, but I hadn't expected it to happen so soon. We found the entire pride gathered around the kill, having already spent many hours feasting. The sight and the experience of being so close was breathtaking. From a few meters away, I witnessed the lions interact with each other and battle for the best pieces of fresh meat.

I left Dinokeng Game Reserve after breakfast, slowly driving along the natural road one last time, witnessing the beauty of the place and saying goodbye to the animals I encountered on the way to the main gate. I love the feeling of not knowing what lies ahead, moving in harmony with a Greater Intelligence and the guidance I receive. It is as though I am following the signs and direction that life puts in front of me, and trusting that the Universe always has my back, even when

FIRST EXCURSION TO SOUTH AFRICA

I'm uncertain of what comes next. There is something extremely beautiful about being in the wilderness that parallels the human experience in a profound way. I felt it this time, just as I have felt it every other time I have been in the wilderness, especially the African wilderness.

The trip back to Warsaw, though quite lengthy, was smooth, and I felt like I was returning from one of the most memorable holidays of my life. I felt a little tired, but having experienced so much of what I had dreamt of, I carried an undercurrent of fulfillment and joy.

CHAPTER 5

LONDOLOZI GAME RESERVE

I was curious about the other part of the country, so I researched it and learned that there is a convenient flight connection between Cape Town and Skukuza in the Sabi Sand Nature Reserve, where I was to be picked up by Londolozi staff. I had been looking forward to this event for more than six months, excited to be in the presence of traditional Shangaan trackers. During one of my conversations with the couple from whom I was renting a cottage, I mentioned the main reason for my visit to South Africa and briefly shared my two greatest passions:

explorative traveling and writing. The man, upon hearing this, looked at me and said, "That sounds similar to what Paul Theroux does," and brought out one of his books titled *The Safari of a Black Star,* which I found in a bookstore a few weeks later.

Upon my arrival at the Skukuza airport, I was warmly welcomed by two staff members from Londolozi Game Reserve. It was a beautiful, sunny, warm day, and the experience that I had been looking forward to was about to begin. After a brief introductory conversation in front of the main hall, we picked up our luggage, piled into the vehicle, and drove to the camp, which was about forty-five minutes from the airport. As I observed the richness of wildlife in their natural habitat, I immediately experienced a familiar sense of joy.

LONDOLOZI GAME RESERVE

One of the most memorable moments at Londolozi was the day we tracked lions. We met early in the morning, having already been told that we would be tracking them. As we drove through the darkness of the bush to greet the day, we heard a distant roar. We spent the entire morning attempting to locate the source of the roar, but the animals were constantly moving and crossed the border into neighboring land that we couldn't enter, so we had to change the direction of our search. A little later, we found fresh lion tracks and, as they became more visible, the senior tracker took over, guiding us with even more focused energy. The experience intensified as he sped up significantly, his movements becoming focused and alert. We were asked to be completely silent, slow down, and lower our backs. We stopped behind a small tree. About a hundred meters ahead, we spotted a pair of lions calmly lying on the grass and silently looking in our direction.

We spent one of the nights in Londolozi in the bush, where it is essential to maintain constant vigilance. Although animals tend to stay away from fire, they are curious and may approach if they think they have a chance to get something to eat. For that reason, we took turns keeping watch in ninety-minute shifts throughout the night. My shift was calm and nothing interesting happened. I tended the fire, scanned the dark surroundings, and sat in the most pristine silence I had ever experienced. In the morning, I learned that during one of the other shifts, a hyena had walked around the camp trying to get some food. As we were leaving the camp, we also noticed traces at the edge of the firelight where a lioness and at least one cub had been watching us from a distance in the darkness of the night.

Those few days in Londolozi passed in a strange way—very fast and very slow at the same time. By the end of the trip, it felt like a galaxy had gone by since the initial day, yet when the final morning arrived, I felt like the retreat had passed very quickly.

CHAPTER 6

NAMIBIA

During my trip to Namibia, I realized very quickly why my experiences during my last two excursions to South Africa unfolded in the way they did. It became clear that those experiences were gradually preparing me for what was to come.

It's a strange experience to wake up in a tent on the roof of your car in the middle of the bush, surrounded by the vast landscape of a foreign country. With gradual steps forward, taking care of the necessary tasks around the camp, I began to gain confidence, which lessened my sense of bewilderment. After familiarizing myself with the equipment and getting used to the way it functioned, one of the first things I did was go for a morning game drive. The place I chose, though quite close to the capital of the country, had a huge, fenced area of land divided into two sections accessible by off-road vehicle.

For the first few days, I drove around the entire property, watching the mostly unafraid giraffes that were present in huge numbers, herds of wildebeests that ran away the minute they spotted someone coming, countless impalas migrating across the land, the ever present but—due to their color—mostly invisible kudus, and small families of warthogs that showed up here and there. On the third morning, I drove to Etosha National Park, which was a few hours away from my first location. The first day in that place I rested from my trip and got used to spending my days around the camp.

NAMIBIA

This was also when I started to break down my daily activities, and the process of getting used to a new environment, with regular writing sessions.

The next few days followed a similar pattern as I tried to find balance between game drives and resting at the camp. After just three days at this location, I was on the road again. This time, the journey was much longer and more demanding. I took the road about eight hundred kilometers north toward Rundu and the Kavango region. Along the way, I experienced waves of wonder at the beauty of landscapes I had never seen before, mixed with waves of anxiety when I allowed my thoughts to drift too far into the future or indulge in doubts about what I was doing.

The way I was traveling across Namibia is known as overlanding. Overlanding, in its simplest form, refers to moving across the land with equipment that enables the traveler's independence. When overlanding, the journey itself is more important than reaching a certain destination. As soon as my bewilderment faded and I was able to orient myself, the sense of adventure I experienced was enormous. After a few days in Namibia, while in Etosha National Park, I began to feel that this was exactly what my soul wanted me to be doing. I began to see it with my eyes. I began to see it on my face. I began to feel it in my heart.

After almost three weeks in Namibia, I decided to return to the first camp where I had stayed after my arrival. My plan, as it evolved, was to fly from Windhoek to Maun in Botswana, rent a car, and drive to the Moremi Game Reserve. The next morning, I drove to the bush via a longer loop that was about twenty kilometers in length. I encountered several large herds of giraffes, many impalas, a few oryxes living in pairs that ran away the minute they noticed the approaching car, and one large herd of wildebeest that all stared at my vehicle with intense focus from about three hundred meters away before running away with steady energy and disappearing into the bush. Initially, I though the longer loop would be enough for me, and I would return to camp after completing the loop, but as soon as I finished, I drove straight into the second loop. It was slightly more challenging and demanded more focus. Slowly and carefully, I drove over numerous bumps and holes, between rocks, across the deep sands of a dry river, through hills, and along gravel roads full of small stones that hit the car's chassis.

The following morning, as soon as I woke up, I went for a short walk to the bush. It was just before the sunrise and the night was slowly fading away, gradually making way for a new day to begin.

AJCUNA

I started walking along the trail that led from the camp to the bushes, allowing me to explore this unique land on foot. The further I walked, the brighter the morning became. I was already on my way back to camp when I was stopped by one of the most beautiful sights I have ever witnessed. It was a small giraffe looking at me from between the bushes. She was so silent that I barely noticed her. I watched the animal as she slowly walked a few meters away toward the bushes, turned around, and looked at me. We stared at each other for few moments, before she walked the next few meters, turned around to look at me once more, and then gracefully ran away, disappearing between the trees.

My initial plan was to drop off the rental car in Windhoek. However, the feedback from the car rental company in Botswana hadn't yet arrived, so I

NAMIBIA

extended my stay at the camp for a few more nights. It seemed wise to exercise some patience and wait for things to happen naturally rather than pushing too hard. Eventually, I received a response from the main office of the car rental company, informing me that the office in Maun was experiencing technical issues, which they hoped to resolve soon so they could process my request. The next morning, just after breakfast, I received an email from the rental company with a form to complete and return to finalize my booking. As there was no printer at the camp, I had to drive to Okahandja, print the form, fill it out, and send back to the Maun office. Everything went smoothly, and I returned to camp thinking that my departure was becoming increasingly possible. As moved around the camp, I was a bit concerned that the car rental company hadn't replied yet, so I decided to follow up and ask how things were going. I checked my email, only to discover that the form had been sent to a printing company instead of the car rental company. The milestone was when a lady from the Maun office recalculated my rental fee to an amount that felt reasonable. From that moment on, even though something was telling me to keep going, I felt that the Universe had given me the green light to move forward, and that it was safe to purchase a flight ticket to Maun.

CHAPTER 7

MOREMI GAME RESERVE

The minute the plane began its descent and reached an altitude low enough for me to see land, I instantly felt a sense of aliveness and enthusiasm. I was amazed and surprised by my change in my mood from tiredness and fogginess to a renewed energy. As soon as I saw the bush below, I straightened my back and felt something pulling me forward, as though there was magnetic force between my chest and Botswana. The moment I met the man from the car rental company, I felt the current of life take over, as though I was meant to come to this place, meet this man, and carry on by myself into the wilderness.

One evening before I departed for the Moremi Reserve, I was sitting on my tent's veranda when I found an off-road magazine that had caught my attention so entirely a few weeks earlier at a gas station in Poland. I looked down at the magazine's cover, then up at the picturesque landscape in front me, and realized that they were remarkably similar sights—both featuring the same car adapted to off-road conditions.

It was afternoon at South Gate Campsite. Since I arrived in Africa, I had begun to lose sense of what day of the week it was. This didn't matter much, but what did matter was the pace of each day, which was defined by the number of tasks I needed to complete to feel comfortable and ensure my daily functioning. As I moved through the Moremi Game

Reserve each day, witnessing wild animals in their natural habitat and noticing its abundance of elephants, hippos, impalas, zebras, kudus, waterbucks, giraffes, and birds, I realized that this was the actualization of something I had been guided toward during the past year. Everything around me at that time was the result of following the guidance, signs, intuitions, bodily sensations, and synchronicities that had been presented to me. Everything that had drawn my attention and sparked my curiosity about the African continent, its wildlife, explorative traveling, and creative expression through writing, led me to this particular moment when the experiences were no longer in the realm of dreams or images, but had become the tangible reality around me.

I passed through Khwai village and continued over a bridge made of huge tree trunks laid together, which made all sorts of noises each time vehicle crossed, but allowed for a slow yet safe passage over the river. When I finally arrived at the campsite booking office, I found it closed. I parked the car and walked around, spotting the familiar faces of my South African neighbors from the Moghoto Campsite. We began talking about our experiences at the Moremi Reserve and exchanging insights, and I explained why I was traveling alone. Then, the lady from the campsite office returned and helped me with my booking.

The next morning, in order not to disturb my neighbors after their unexpected arrival the night before, I rose as silently as possible, packed my tent, brushed my teeth, and headed over to the bush. My intuition was heightened, guiding me through a number of dirt roads across the open terrains of this part of the reserve, until I arrived at an area thick with bushes right off the main road. In front of me, lying in the middle of the road, was an entire pride of lions. Most of them were still sleeping, and at first, I couldn't tell how large the pride was. I carefully and slowly drove closer, stopping my vehicle about sixty meters in front of them. Some lions raised their heads to look at the car, while others remained indifferent. From my perspective, I could see lionesses and a few cubs lying close by, either sleeping or slowly waking up to new day. A few minutes later, I noticed the massive head of young male rising from the grass, as if he wanted to check what was happening. The lion slowly looked around a few times, before hiding his head again. The longer I stayed there, the more of them I could spot. After some time, the pride began to make slow movements, seemingly searching for a more comfortable and less sunny place to continue their morning rest. One of the cubs moved closer to a lioness and began playing with her, teasing and jumping around. At some point, the male stood up, walked toward the pride, passed by them, and lay down in the shade close to the bush.

Later that day, after spending some time back at camp, I returned to the same spot to see if the lions were still there. Knowing that lions spend most of their day sleeping, resting, and searching for shade, I expected they might still be there—if not in the exact spot, then somewhere nearby. I couldn't see them as I first approached, but they were still there—hidden, lying next to each other in the thick bush, hardly visible at first glance. I had to drive closer to see their bright hair and the shapes of the animals sleeping amid the heat of the day. I returned one more time later that afternoon, though I was quite certain they would have moved to another location by then. I could barely see through the bushes, but I recognized that they were still inside. As I couldn't see much, I decided to drive around a thick bunch of small trees for a better vantage point. As I turned deeper into the bush, I saw a huge lioness lying with her cub. She was completely indifferent to the presence of the vehicle and hardly paid me any attention, even though I was only about three meters away. The cub was sleeping with his head between her legs, occasionally raising his head to see what was happening around him. Up close, the lioness was huge, much larger than I had imagined. The moment I started to back the car out of the bushes, the cub raised his head, stared directly at the moving car, and placed his large paw on the sleeping lioness, as if concerned about what was happening.

CHAPTER 8

BEING BACK IN POLAND

During the final days of working on my book in Poland, further guidance and my next destination unexpectedly revealed itself to me during a walk in the park. I sensed that, after spending more than two months in Poland, a place that beautifully served the purpose of completing this book, I may soon embark on another adventure. The next destination emerged in one of those moments where, if we are sensitive, attentive, and present enough, we can notice what life is currently trying to communicate and invite us toward. We have the opportunity to step into a new direction already destined for us, guiding us closer to a life in alignment with our purpose and the fulfillment of our potential.

ACKNOWLEDGMENTS

This book would not have been possible without the support of several people at different stages of its creation. First, I would like to say thank you to Kathy Meis for her professionalism, publishing expertise, responsiveness, and guidance from the moment we met. I also extend my thanks to the various teams involved in this creative process, including Anne and Shilah, for keeping the project together.

I thank my mother for her support during the final stages of writing and preparing the book for publication. I am deeply grateful to Boyd Varty for inspiring me and introducing me to the ancient art of tracking. I would like to express my gratitude to Martha Beck for her guidance in helping me connect with the most essential and natural parts of myself, and for providing the numerous tools that have helped me pursue my dreams.

AUTHOR BIOGRAPHY

Marcin Kozakowski, born in Warsaw, Poland, is a dedicated explorer of self-discovery and spiritual growth. Over the past eight years, Marcin has passionately pursued a life of harmony with Greater Intelligence, blending his innate gifts and talents with a deep commitment to healing and personal reinvention. His journey has included transformative experiences, such as a South African retreat where he studied the ancient art of tracking with world-class experts, solo overlanding excursions through Namibia and Botswana, and explorations from Ghana through Ethiopia to Malawi and

Zimbabwe. Through his writing, Marcin hopes to inspire readers to see that a life of unique fulfillment is within reach.

www.ingramcontent.com/pod-product-compliance
Lightning Source LLC
Chambersburg PA
CBHW052207070526
44585CB00017B/2098